WORLD 1990 SPECIAL

© 1990 Grandreams Limited

Edited by
John Barraclough.

Layout and design by
Nigel I. Money.

Researched, compiled and written by
Tony Lynch.

All photographs supplied by and are copyright, Allsport.

Published January 1990 by

GRANDREAMS LIMITED,
Jadwin House,
205/211 Kentish Town Road,
London NW5 2JU.

Printed in Belgium.

ISBN 0 86227 737 X

For four weeks this summer twenty-four nations representing the cream of international soccer will compete in the fourteenth World Cup Finals.

In a feast of football fifty-two matches will be played at twelve venues all over Italy, culminating in the Final itself at the magnificent Olympic Stadium in Rome, on Sunday July 8.

This Grandreams Special previews all the contenders and assesses their chances of success. We also spotlight the stars and take a look back at past World Cup Finals.

The centre pages feature a terrific World Cup Chart on which you can record the progress of the tournament.

AND you could win a 14" portable colour TV in our great, free to enter competition!

Preparing for the world's premier soccer tournament has been...

A MONUMENTAL TASK

Three times winners of the World Cup and home to some of the most successful clubs in Europe, Italy is one of the world's proudest soccer playing nations.

But, ever since it was decided that Italy would host the 1990 Finals there has been an extra buzz of excitement and anticipation all over the country.

There has been a great deal of hard work in the twelve specially selected venues where the tournament will be played. And there have been more than a few headaches, caused largely by the kind of political and beaurocratic difficulties for which Italy has long been renowned.

The burning question most frequently asked in Italian football circles has been: Will we be ready? Ensuring that the answer is a resounding "YES" has been the job of Luca di Montezemolo, director and general manager of the Italia '90 organising committee.

Heading a team of 160 dedicated administrators, it has been Montezemolo's monumental task to see that the 1990 World Cup Finals will run smoothly and will ultimately be a resounding success.

The first priority has been the preparation of the twelve stadia, situated in various and diverse regions of the country. Each was to become a comfortable all-seater venue.

In most cases this meant the redevelopment and refurbishment of existing grounds. Rome's Olympic Stadium, for example, was closed in the summer of '89 (much to the annoyance of joint-owners, Roma and Lazio, who were forced to play 'home' matches in the much smaller Flaminio Stadium nearby).

In Turin an exciting, brand new stadium, The Nuovo Comunale, has been built, with a seating capacity of 70,000.

Sadly, two tragedies occurred during work on the stadia. In August, 1989, five workmen were killed when eleven steel supports collapsed during construction of the roof of the Della Favorita Stadium in Palermo. Then, just a few weeks later, a drainage trench collapsed during work on the Turin stadium. One worker was killed in the incident. In view of these accidents safety measures were tightened up at all the redevelopment sites.

While the twelve stadiums were being made ready, the Italia '90 organising team had a whole host of other arrangements to make.

Suitable hotels and training centres had to be selected for each of the twenty-three visiting squads. A

Opposite page above: The Sant' Elia Stadium in Cagliari where England will play all their group games. Below: The Comunale Stadium, Florence.

2

3

The splendour of the World Cup draw which took place in Rome, December, 1989.

glossy brochure, detailing just what was on offer, was produced and distributed among the qualifiers.

Similarly, matchday facilities had to be arranged for the vast army of over 2000 journalists and photographers who will be covering the tournament.

Worldwide TV coverage had to be carefully planned. This involved the building of a new production centre close to the Olympic Stadium in Rome - and the launching of a new satellite to beam the pictures around the globe. It is estimated that the total TV audience will be around 16 billion.

Policing and security is a major factor in the running of any football tournament, particularly with today's ever-present threat of hooliganism hanging over the game. A policy has been drawn up to deal quickly and efficiently with any troublemakers.

Likewise, a computer network has been set up linking the Italian authorities to Football's ruling bodies throughout the world. It is hoped that by international co-operation known troublemakers will be weeded-out at the ticket-buying stage.

Of course, the influx of millions of visitors to the World Cup Finals will provide a great boost to the already successful Italian tourist industry. To deal with this a number of new hotels are hoping to open their doors in time for the tournament.

The World Cup draw which took place in Rome's Palazzo dello Sport on December 9, 1989, was seen by an estimated 500 million people in 58 countries.

Italian celebrities - Sophia Loren (dubbed 'The Godmother of the World Cup'), Luciano Pavarotti and George Moroder assisted with the draw as did a handful of ex-World Cup stars including Bobby Moore, Bruno Conti and Pele. The ceremony was accompanied by clips from twelve short films made by a dozen of Italy's top directors. Each extolled the virtues of one of the tournament's venues - and will be shown in full throughout the competition.

Top film and opera director Franco Zeffirelli has been commissioned to produce the actual opening ceremony in Rome, which will feature a spectacular Olympic-style parade.

When that is over, the tournament will begin - and Luca di Montezemolo and his team will be hoping that their organisational efforts will be matched by some fabulous football.

THE VENUES

GROUP C
GENOA Luigi Ferraris Stadium - Capacity 40,000
TURIN Nuovo Comunale Stadium - Capacity 70,000

GROUP D
MILAN San Siro Stadium - Capacity 80,000
BOLOGNA Renato Dell' Ara Stadium - Capacity 46,000

GROUP E
VERONA Marc Antonio Bentegodi Stadium - Capacity 44,000
UDINE Friuli Stadium - Capacity 40,000

GROUP B
NAPLES San Paolo Stadium - Capacity 75,000
BARI Della Vittoria Stadium - Capacity 58,000

GROUP A
FLORENCE Comunale Stadium - Capacity 61,000
ROME Olympic Stadium - Capacity 83,000

GROUP F
CAGLIARI Sant' Elia Stadium - Capacity 45,000
PALERMO Della Favorita Stadium - Capacity 38,000

THE HOSTS

Italy

Group A

National Colours: *Blue shirts, white shorts, blue socks with red and white trim*

Change Colours: *White shirts with pale blue stripe, blue shorts, blue socks.*

National Stadium: *Olympic Stadium, Rome*

Automatic qualification as host nation.

"Thanks Brazil, You Taught Us A Lesson!" - that was the sporting headline in an Italian national newspaper after the Italy-Brazil friendly played in Bologna last October. Without fielding a full-strength squad Brazil had dominated the proceedings and had won the match with a single goal, scored by substitute Andre Cruz in the 77th minute.

The following month saw the Italians continuing their World Cup preparations with a friendly against England at Wembley. Although the game ended in a 0-0 stalemate, England effectively ruled the roost. Both of these results gave Italian manager Azeglio Vicini much food for thought.

His squad which had performed well in reaching the semi-finals of the '88 European Championships, seemed to be suffering a touch of pre-World Cup nerves. The question now is: will the Italians get their act together in time for the finals?

Vicini certainly has enough talent to choose from,

in all departments. Walter Zenga is regarded as one of the top goalkeepers in the world and is well protected by the defensive might of Giuseppi Bergomi, Franco Baresi (injury and personal problems permitting!), Riccardo Ferri, Ciro Ferrara and company.

The midfield boasts Fernando De Napoli, and the dynamic little Giuseppi Giannini. In attack is the lethal striker Gianluca Vialli (whose style has been likened to England's Bobby Charlton of old) and the exciting Roberto Baggio, hailed as Italy's most talented find in years.

If these aces and their team-mates can rediscover their touch this summer then the Italian fans, bred on international success and used to one of the most glamorous league competitions in the world, will be more than happy.

World Cup nerves or not, Italy must surely rank among the firm favourites for the title - simply because they enjoy home advantage.

Opposite page top: Walter Zenga, rated one of the world's top 'keepers. Opposite page bottom: Ginaluca Vialli; Italy's Bobby Charlton? This page: Giuseppi Giannini, Italy's midfield maestro.

THE CHAMPIONS

Argentina

Group B

National Colours: *Pale blue and white striped shirts, black shorts, white socks.*

Change Colours: *Dark blue shirts, white shorts, white socks.*

National Stadium: *River Plate Stadium, Buenos Aires.*

1986 World Cup Winners Automatic Qualification

Twice winners of the World Cup, once runners-up - that's Argentina's proud record. But it is one they will be aiming to improve upon in 1990, for the Argentinean fans will not be satisfied until their national team has emulated the trio of World Championship wins achieved by neighbouring Brazil. The Argentineans are also desperate to win the World Cup in a tournament held in Europe, the 'away' continent: only Brazil have ever achieved that feat (in Sweden in 1958).

Something else that rankles with them at the moment is the fact that Brazil are the current holders of the 'Copa America' - the South American Championship (Argentina finished third behind Uruguay).

All-in-all the 1986 World Cup winners have a great deal to prove and a lot to live up to in Italy.

As current holders they automatically qualify for the finals. But that is not necessarily a good thing. Past champions walking straight into the finals have sometimes experienced a loss of the competitive edge that comes with the rigours of qualifying. No amount of friendly games played in preparation can provide an

8

adequate substitute for the real thing. Allied to this is the fact that Argentina have had to virtually rebuild the side that won the World Cup in '86.

But they still have Diego Maradona. The star of the 1986 finals now enjoys a millionaire lifestyle and plys his trade in the Italian League. Despite problems - now resolved - with his club Napoli, he is still rated as one of the best players in the world and, if he can find that extra touch of magic, he could well inspire his team-mates to Argentina's third World Championship. He even has the advantage of playing two Group B qualifying games (against the USSR and Romania) on his club ground in Naples.

Opposite page: Claudio Caniggia, left: Nery Pumpido and above: the brilliant and explosive Diego Maradona. Can these 3 stars help Argentina retain the trophy that they won in Mexico 1986?

Austria

Group A

National Colours: *White shirts, black shorts, black socks.*

Change Colours: *Red shirts, white shorts, red socks*

National Stadium: *Wiener, Vienna.*

European Qualifying Group Three

	P	W	D	L	F	A	Pts
USSR	8	4	3	1	11	4	11
AUSTRIA	**8**	**3**	**3**	**2**	**9**	**9**	**9**
Turkey	8	3	1	4	12	10	7
E. Germany	8	3	1	4	9	13	7
Iceland	8	1	4	3	6	11	6

Austria qualified for Italia '90 in great style. In the final deciding match of their campaign, they beat fellow contenders East Germany 3-0. The highlight of the game was a superb hat-trick by Toni Polster - definitely a striker to watch out for in Italy. That result gave Austria the runners-up spot in the European Qualifying Group Three behind the USSR, and takes them to their fifth World Cup.

Austria has, in fact, a fine footballing tradition stretching back to 1902 when they played Hungary in the very first international to be staged outside Great Britain. The Austrians won that game 5-0. In the 1930's they became known as the 'Wunderteam' and in 1934 they finished fourth in the World Cup held in Italy. In the 1954 tournament in Switzerland, they finished third behind West Germany and Hungary.

Although qualifying for the 1978 and 1982 World Cup Finals, the Austrians have since failed to make much of an impression on the international scene - until now. The splendid World Cup run has breathed new life into the game all over the country.

They were perhaps unfortunate in being drawn in the same group as Italy, but still have a good chance of progressing to the second phase.

Anton Polster, whose hat-trick against East Germany secured Austria's qualification, will give defences plenty to think about in Italy.

Led by veteran manager Guy Thys, Belgium were the surprise packet of the 1986 World Cup, finishing in fourth place behind Argentina, West Germany and France.

One of the highlights of that campaign was little Belgium's spirited defeat of the mighty USSR in the second round. Indeed, it was arguably the most exciting game of the tournament. After 90 minutes the scoreline stood at 2-2 with the Russians looking decidedly the stronger of the two sides. But the Belgians fought like tigers to win the game 4-3. Extra-time was needed in their quarter-final encounter against Spain, but the match went to a penalty shoot-out with Belgium eventually winning 5-4.

But the Belgian bubble burst in the semi-finals when they were soundly beaten by Argentina. They then went on to lose the Third Place match against France. Nevertheless, the squad returned home to a real heroes' welcome.

After that the Belgian game seemed to suffer for a while. Surprisingly they failed to qualify for the 1988 European Championships, a fact attributed to the retirement of Thys whose inspirational leadership and wise tactical sense had been a major factor in reaching the dizzy heights of '86.

Now, new manager Walter Meeuws has steered his team back on course again. They made it to Italia '90 by topping the European Group Seven in the qualifying tournament - and they were seeded on their past World Cup record.

With stars like striker Jan Ceulemans, attacking full back Patrick Vervoort and 'keeper Michel Preud'homme Belgium should qualify from Group E and then once again prove to be a thorn in the sides of the bigger nations.

Jan Ceulemans, a regular in the Belgium side for over a decade. His vision has helped his side produce many a shock.

Belgium

Group E

National Colours: *All red, with black, yellow and red trim.*

Change Colours: *All white.*

National Stadium: *Heysel, Brussels.*

European Qualifying Group Seven

	P	W	D	L	F	A	Pts
BELGIUM	8	4	4	0	15	5	12
Czechoslovakia	8	5	2	1	13	3	12
Portugal	8	4	2	2	11	8	10
Switzerland	8	2	1	5	10	14	5
Luxembourg	8	0	1	7	3	22	1

Brazil

Group C

National Colours: *Yellow shirts with green trim, blue shorts, white socks.*

Change Colours: *Blue shirts, white shorts, white socks.*

National Stadium: *Maracana, Rio de Janeiro.*

South American Qualifying Group Three

	P	W	D	L	F	A	Pts
BRAZIL	4	3	1	0	12	2	7
Chile	4	2	1	1	9	4	5
Venezuela	4	0	0	4	2	17	0

The brilliant Brazilians reckon it's time they won the World Cup again. The last time that happened was twenty years ago - way back in 1970 when they beat Italy 4-1 in Mexico. That emphatic victory was Brazil's third World Cup triumph - a feat which earned them possession of the Jules Rimet Trophy for all time.

That was in the days of such great Brazilian stars as Gerson, Rivelino, Carlos Alberto, Jairzinho - and of course, everyone's favourite player, the magical Pele.

Since then the Brazilians, still regarded as the most skilful ball-players in the world, have remained the best of all possible crowd-pullers on the international scene. But in terms of success they have found themselves somewhat eclipsed by South American rivals Argentina.

All of that could be about to change. Last year Brazil won the 'Copa America' - the South American Championship - beating Uruguay 1-0 in Rio de Janeiro, before a crowd of 178,000. As far as the Brazilian fans are concerned that's almost (almost, but not quite!) as good as winning the World Cup itself.

Brazil's route to Italy was tinged with controversy. The outcome of their South American qualifying group boiled down to the final match against Chile, played in Rio. Brazil were 2-0 ahead when all hell seemed to break loose. With firecrackers exploding and the Chilean goalkeeper, Rojas, claiming that he had be struck by a flare thrown from the crowd, the Chileans stormed off the field. A FIFA enquiry later ruled that the scoreline should stand, Rojas was heavily fined by his own FA and Brazil went through to the finals.

Now, Brazil's star-studded line-up - which includes Romario, Babeto, Silas, Dunga, Muller and £3 Million Man Careca (probably the best striker in the world at the moment) - will be more determined than ever to put their country back at the top of world football.

With their pedigree, they might well succeed.

Branco (left) and Romario (above) are just two members of a star-studded Brazilian side that are hoping to achieve World Cup success for the fourth time in Italy.

Cameroon

Group B

National Colours: *Green shirts, red shorts, yellow socks.*

National Stadium: *Ahamadou Ahijo, Yaounde*

African Qualifying Tournament Group C

	P	W	D	L	F	A	Pts
CAMEROON	6	4	1	1	9	6	9
Nigeria	6	3	1	2	7	5	7
Angola	6	1	2	3	6	7	4
Gabon	6	2	0	4	5	9	4

Play-off matches: CAMEROON 2, Tunisia 0 Tunisia 0, CAMEROON 1. Cameroon won 3-0 on aggregate

Mbouh of Cameroon goes past the Tunisian defence.

Cameroon, who will open the 1990 World Cup Finals against Argentina on June 8, have long been regarded as one of Africa's best soccer nations and are considered the strongest of the 'minnow' teams in Italy.

In 1982 they qualified for the World Cup Finals in Spain and drew all three of their opening round games against such strong opposition as Poland, Italy and Peru. Unfortunately, three points were not enough to take them through to the next stage. But Cameroon had made a remarkable debut on the world stage.

Now they are back for a second attempt, having gained one of the two African berths in Italy. An incredible 85,000 crowd turned out to watch the first play-off match against Tunisia in Yaounde, last October.

Other qualifiers be warned. Cameroon could perform even better than they did in '82. Players to watch out for are Emmanuel Kunde and Louis-Paul Mfede.

Costa Rica

Group C

National Colours: *Red shirts, blue shorts, white socks.*

National Stadium: *National, Explanada De La Sabana.*

CONCACAF Qualifying Group

	P	W	D	L	F	A	Pts
COSTA RICA	8	5	1	2	10	8	11
U.S.A.	8	4	3	1	6	3	11
Trinidad & Tobago	8	3	3	2	7	5	9
Guatemala	6	1	1	4	4	7	3*
El Salvador	6	0	2	4	2	8	2*

* Guatemala and El Salvador did not complete their programme of matches

By October 1989 Costa Rica's place at Italia '90 was mathematically assured. Their position among the first two qualifying spots in the CONCACAF group was unassailable.

It was a campaign which had included a second round walk-over against Mexico, who were banned for two years from taking part in international football at any level following an 'age fixing' scandal in the run up to the World Youth Cup Finals.

It is true to say that had the Mexicans played, then the outcome of the entire CONCACAF group would probably have been quite different. As it happened they were a major obstacle removed.

However, that is not to detract from the achievements of Costa Rica - they deserve to be in Italy on merit. But now they must take on three particularly strong teams - Brazil, Sweden and Scotland - and are unlikely to progress beyond the first round.

Montero of Costa Rica. His team face a tough task in their group matches against Brazil, Sweden and Scotland.

Football in Colombia has undergone something of a major reorganisation during the last ten years. What was once considered a rather slapdash approach has now become a serious business extending through every level of the game - from schoolboys right up to the big clubs such as Nacional and Medellin.

Two seasons ago they came to Britain to play in the Rous Cup tournament - and creditable draws with Scotland and England won them a great deal of respect.

To reach the Italia '90 finals Colombia had first to top their South American qualifying group, ahead of Ecuador and Paraguay. But that wasn't all - they then had to beat Israel, winners of the Oceania group, in a two-leg play-off.

If stars like Arnaldo Iguaran, Albeiro Uzurriaga and the terrifically talented, but often temperamental Carlos Valderrama are on song, then Colombia could produce some of the finest football of the summer and could even spring a surprise or two.

Carlos Valderrama, the talented but often temperamental star of Colombia.

Colombia

Group D

National Colours: *Red shirts, blue shorts, red socks.*

Change Colours: *Yellow shirts, blue shorts, red socks.*

National Stadium: *El Campin, Bogota.*

South American Qualifying Group Two

	P	W	D	L	F	A	Pts
COLOMBIA	4	2	1	1	5	3	5
Paraguay	4	2	0	2	6	7	4
Ecuador	4	1	1	2	4	5	3

Play-off with Oceania Group winners, Israel COLOMBIA 1, Israel 0. Israel 0, COLOMBIA 0. Colombia won 1-0 on aggregate

The Czechs are no strangers to the World Cup stage, having qualified seven times before 1990 and twice being runners-up in the competition. In the 1934 final, in Rome, Czechoslovakia were a goal up against Italy with just nine minutes left to play - but the Italians stormed back to equalise and then take the game 2-1 after extra-time.

In 1962 the Czechs won through to the final in Chile where they met Brazil. Once again they took the lead in a World Cup Final, with a goal by the inspirational Josef Masopust. But the Brazilians were at their magical best and eventually won the game 3-1.

Czechoslovakia became European Champions in 1976 when they beat West Germany after a penalty shoot-out in Yugoslavia. Since then they have qualified for just one World Cup Finals, in Spain in 1982, but failed to get beyond the opening round.

Czechoslovakia qualified for Italia '90 by finishing as runners-up to Belgium in the closely-fought European Group Seven campaign. Both teams had twelve points and an equal goal difference, but Belgium topped the table with a higher goals for tally.

It was tough going for the Czechs, particularly in their first game against Portugal. Michal Bilek put Czechoslovakia ahead with a penalty after 11 minutes. Seven minutes later they were reduced to ten men when Griga was sent off. Portugese pressure produced an equaliser in the 74th minute. But then the remarkable Bilek got the winner from a curling free kick in the 82nd minute.

Other Czech stars to watch out for in Italy are midfield mastermind Ivan Hasek and goal-getter Vaclav Nemecek.

Czechoslovakia's Frantisek Staka.

Czechoslovakia

Group A

National Colours: *Red shirts, white shorts, blue socks.*

Change Colours: *All white.*

National Stadium: *Central Army Stadium, Prague.*

European Qualifying Group Seven

	P	W	D	L	F	A	Pts
Belgium	8	4	4	0	15	5	12
CZECHOSLOVAKIA	8	5	2	1	13	3	12
Portugal	8	4	2	2	11	8	10
Switzerland	8	2	1	5	10	14	5
Luxembourg	8	0	1	7	3	22	1

Egypt

Egypt's talented Hany Ramzy.

Group F

National Colours: Red shirts, white shorts, black socks

National Stadium: Nasser, Cairo.

African Qualifying Tournament Group B

EGYPT	P	W	D	L	F	A	Pts
	6	3	2	1	6	2	8
Liberia	6	2	2	2	3	6	
Malawi	6	1	3	2	3	4	5
Kenya	6	1	3	2	2	4	5

The victories that have taken Egypt to the World Cup Finals were all recorded at home, so they will find it very tough going indeed in Italy. It is doubtful that they will survive against Group F opponents England, Holland and the Republic of Ireland. But that won't spoil the fun for the Egyptian fans whose side have made it to the World Cup Finals for the first time in their history. They got there by qualifying for one of the two African places, along with Cameroon. Players to watch out for are Abdelhamid, El Kas and Hassan.

England

Group F

National Colours: *White shirts, Blue shorts, white socks.*

Change Colours: *Red shirts, white shorts, red socks.*

National Stadium: *Wembley, London.*

European Qualifying Group Two

	P	W	D	L	F	A	Pts
Sweden	6	4	2	0	9	3	10
ENGLAND	6	3	3	0	10	0	9
Poland	6	2	1	3	4	8	5
Albania	6	0	0	6	3	15	0

Left: Bryan Robson, England's inspirational skipper. Right above: Gary Lineker, seen here in action against Poland, was top scorer in Mexico. His form will be a vital factor if England are to find success in the sunshine.

Right below: Peter Shilton saves during England's quarter-final match against Argentina in Mexico '86.

England's World Cup campaign began at Wembley against Sweden just four months after their dismal display in the 1988 European Championships. After that poor showing there really was only one way to go - up!

Yet that first game proved a disappointing 0-0 draw and it looked as if Bobby Robson had yet to iron out his problems. Then two relatively easy ties against the charming, but naive, Albanians produced an expected crop of goals - seven in all.

A great all-round team performance - England's best of the campaign - secured a 3-0 home victory over Poland with goals from Gary Lineker, John Barnes and Neil Webb. The future suddenly looked very bright indeed. Little did we know that England would score no more goals in the qualifying round.

The well ran dry in the return fixture with the spirited Swedes, and England were lucky to get away with a 0-0 draw. The dominant feature of this game was Terry Butcher's heroic bloodstained performance in the heart of defence.

As it was, a last-minute effort beat Shilton and wobbled the English crossbar - but it did not go in. The scoreline remained at 0-0 and England were placed at the top of the table. However, the importance of Shilton's contribution was underlined two weeks later, when Sweden beat Poland to win the Group Two contest. England were through as one of the two 'second best' sides in the smaller European qualifying groups.

This situation led to the 'seeding' controversy raised by Spain who as Group Six winners claimed that they should be seeded ahead of England in the finals. FIFA eventually resolved the argument in England's favour, by using a points system based on performance over the last two World Cup Finals.

England boss Bobby Robson has now put all the trials and tribulations of qualifying behind him and has been concentrating his efforts on preparing for the finals. But even he wasn't ready for the surprise draw which produced a re-run of England's 1988 European Championship fixtures

By the time the last qualifying match rolled around, England needed a point to be sure of a place in the Italian sunshine. That encounter against Poland, in Katowice, will long live in the memory of English fans as the night when Peter Shilton played the game of his life.

Poland, already out of the running and playing for pride, dominated the match. Their attack forced four world class saves out of Shilton in the first-half. Had any of those shots gone in then the match would undoubtedly have been beyond England's recall and their World Cup place would have teetered on the brink.

19

– against Holland and the Republic of Ireland.

Now we can expect a redoubled effort from Robson's men this summer. The last thing England wants is a repeat performance of the '88 horror story.

The squad will probably include: *Peter Shilton* (Derby County), *Chris Woods* (Rangers), *Dave Beasant* (Chelsea), *Gary Stevens* (Rangers), *Des Walker* (Nottingham Forest), *Terry Butcher* (Rangers), *Stuart Pearce* (Nottingham Forest), *Mark Wright* (Derby County), *Bryan Robson* (Manchester United), *Neil Webb* (Manchester United), *Steve McMahon* (Liverpool), *David Rocastle* (Arsenal), *Paul Gascoigne* (Tottenham Hotspur), *Gary Lineker* (Tottenham Hotspur), *Peter Beardsley* (Liverpool), *John Barnes* (Liverpool), *David Platt* (Aston Villa), *Steve Bull* (Wolves), *Chris Waddle* (Marseille).

Terry Butcher (white shirt), the tower of strength in the heart of England's defence.

Complete the panel when the actual England Squad is announced.

1.	13.
2.	14.
3.	15.
4.	16.
5.	17.
6.	18.
7.	19.
8.	20.
9.	21.
10.	22.
11.	23.
12.	24.

Group F

National Colours: *Orange shirts, white shorts, orange socks.*

Change Colours: *All white.*

National Stadium: *Olympisch Stadion, Amsterdam.*

European Qualifying Group Four

	P	W	D	L	F	A	Pts
HOLLAND	6	4	2	0	8	2	10
West Germany	6	3	3	0	13	3	9
Finland	6	1	1	4	4	16	3
Wales	6	0	2	4	4	8	2

Holland

Holland stands proudly as the reigning European Champions. They won that title in West Germany in the summer of 1988 - and they won it in stunning style.

Who can forget the devastating goal-scoring of Marco van Basten, the fine defending of Frank Rijkaard and Ronald Koeman and the inspired leadership of Ruud Gullit? They were just some of the players who stood out, yet it was really a splendid all-round team performance which culminated in an emphatic 2-0 defeat of the USSR in the final.

Astonishingly enough, the 1988 European Championship earned the Dutch their first ever major international trophy. In the past they had been the 'nearly men' of the World Cup, twice finishing as runners-up: to West Germany in 1974 and to Argentina in 1978. And in 1976 they finished third in the European Championship. All of that happened in the era of 'total football', perfected by manager Rinus Michels and epitomised by such stars as Johan Cruyff and Johan Neeskens.

After those heady days, Dutch football drifted into the international doldrums. They

Ronald Koeman of Holland shows off the European Championship trophy after his team's success in beating the USSR 2-0 in Germany 1988. This win makes Holland one of the favourites for Italy.

failed to qualify for the World Cup Finals of 1982 and 1986. Yet out of those troubled times emerged a new Holland, managed by Michels and led by the flamboyant, dreadlocked Ruud Gullit. His creative talents were valued at more than £5 million when he was transferred from PSV Eindhoven to AC Milan.

Then came 1988 and the Dutch triumph in West Germany. Now, two seasons on, they are asking themselves if they can improve on that triumph?

Amazingly the draw has grouped them with 1988 Euro opponents, England and the Republic of Ireland. Both of those nations will be determined to do better this time around.

Left: Marco van Basten, seen her saluting his goal against England in the 1988 European Championships and below: Ruud Gullit form an explosive striking partnership for the Dutch.

GOING FOR GOLD

Which Super Striker will win the coveted Golden Boot Award, presented to the highest scorer in the World Cup Finals?

Above left: In 1986 England's Gary Lineker was top scorer in Mexico, with six goals. Can he repeat the feat in 1990? Above right: Super-striker Emilio Butregueno, nicknamed 'El Buitre' (The Vulture). He could hold the key to Spanish succes in Italy. Right: How many times will Holland's Marco van Basten find the net in Italy?

Leading Goalscorers

1930
Stabile (Argentina).........6
1934
Schiavo (Italy),
Nejedly (Czechoslovakia),
Conen (Germany)...................4
1938
Leonidas (Brazil)...........8
1950
Ademir (Brazil).............7
1954
Kocsis (Hungary)...........11
1958
Fontaine (France).........13
1962
Jerkovic (Yugoslavia).......5
1966
Eusebio (Portugal).........9
1970
Muller (West Germany)......10
1974
Lato (Poland)...............7
1978
Kempes (Argentina)..........6
1982
Rossi (Italy)...............6
1986
Lineker (England)..........6

WORLD CUP FINALS 1990

FIRST PHASE

	Friday 8 June	Saturday 9 June	Sunday 10 June	Monday 11 June	Tuesday 12 June	Wed. 13 June	Thursday 14 June	Friday 15 June	Saturday 16 June	Sunday 17 June	Monday 18 June	Tuesday 19 June	Wed. 20 June	Thursday 21 June
A Rome Olympico Stadium		Italy v Austria					Italy v USA					Italy v Czech		
Florence Comunale Stadium			USA v Czech.					Austria v Czech.				Austria v USA		
B Naples San Paulo Stadium	Opening Match Argentina					Argentina v USSR					Argentina v Romania			
Bari Della Vittoria Stadium	v Cameroon Milan	USSR v Romania					Cameroon v Romania				Cameroon v USSR			
C Turin Comunale Stadium			Brazil v Sweden						Brazil v Costa Rica				Brazil v Scotland	
Genoa Lugi Ferraris				Costa Rica v. Scotland					Sweden v Scotland				Sweden v. Costa Rica	
D Milan Menazza Stadium			W. Germany v. Yugoslavia					W. Germany v. UAE				W. Germany v. Columbia		
Bologna Renato Dell'Ara		UAE v Columbia					Yugoslavia v. Columbia					Yugoslavia v. UAE		
E Verona Comunale Stadium					Belgium v S. Korea					Belgium v Uruguay				Belgium v Spain
Udine Friuli Stadium						Uruguay v Spain				S. Korea v Spain				S. Korea v Uruguay
F Cagliari Sant'Elia Stadium				England v. Rep. Ireland					England v Holland					England v Egypt
Palermo Della Favorita					Holland v Egypt					Rep. Ireland v. Egypt				Rep. Ireland v. Holland

24

SECOND PHASE

Saturday June 23 **Naples** Kick-off 4.00 pm	B1	Winner from Turin
Saturday June 23 **Bari** Kick-off 8.00pm	A3/C3/D3	Saturday June 30 **Florence** Kick-off 4.00pm
Sunday June 24 **Turin** Kick-off 4.00pm	A2	Winner from Verona
	C2	
Sunday June 24 **Milan** Kick-off 8.00pm	C1	Winner from Genoa
	A3/B3/F3	Saturday June 30 **Rome** Kick-off 8.00pm
Monday June 25 **Genoa** Kick-off 4.00pm	D1	Winner from Rome
	A3/E3/F3	
Monday June 25 **Rome** Kick-off 8.00pm	F2	Winner from Bari
	B2	Sunday July 1 **Milan** Kick-off 4.00pm
Tuesday June 26 **Verona** Kick-off 4.00pm	A1	Winner from Milan
	C3/D3/F3	
Tuesday June 26 **Bologna** Kick-off 8.00pm	E1	Winner from Naples
	D2	Sunday July 1 **Naples** Kick-off 8.00pm
	F1	Winner from Bologna
	E2	

QUARTER FINALS / SEMI FINALS / FINAL

- Tuesday July 3 **Naples** Kick-off 7.00pm
- Wednesday July 4 **Florence** Kick-off 7.00pm
- Sunday July 8 **Rome** Kick-off 7.00pm

3rd PLACE FINAL
Saturday July 7. **Bari**. Kick-off 7.00pm

All times stated are UK local time.

Group Tables

			W	D	L	F	A	Pts
A	1	Italy						
	2	Austria						
	3	USA						
	4	Czechoslovakia						
B	1	Argentina						
	2	Cameroon						
	3	USSR						
	4	Romania						
C	1	Brazil						
	2	Sweden						
	3	Costa Rica						
	4	Scotland						
D	1	W. Germany						
	2	Yugoslavia						
	3	UAE						
	4	Columbia						
E	1	Belgium						
	2	S. Korea						
	3	Uruguay						
	4	Spain						
F	1	England						
	2	Rep. Ireland						
	3	Holland						
	4	Egypt						

Rep. of Ireland

Group F

National Colours: *Green shirts, white shorts, green socks.*

Change Colours: *All white.*

National Stadium: *Lansdowne Road, Dublin* and *Dalymount Park, Dublin.*

European Qualifying Group Six

	P	W	D	L	F	A	Pts
Spain	8	6	1	1	20	3	13
REP. OF IRELAND	8	5	2	1	10	2	12
Hungary	8	2	4	2	8	12	8
N. Ireland	8	2	1	5	6	12	5
Malta	8	0	2	6	3	18	2

Last November five thousand Republic of Ireland fans travelled to Valletta, in Malta. They went there to witness a moment of history in the making. The Republic's national team - managed by an Englishman - needed only a draw to ensure their first ever World Cup Finals appearance.

With a distinct touch of Irish irony it was John Aldridge (he had previously scored just once in 28 international outings) who settled the matter with two well taken goals (one a penalty) in a 2-0 victory.

That night the streets, bars and restaurants of Valletta rang out with the sounds of Irish celebrations. Indeed, the only place where the revellers were more ecstatic and enthusiastic was in Dublin itself. You'd have been forgiven for thinking that the World Cup had already been won by the Boys in Green!

Whether that is a realistic possibility or not, it is true to say that ever since Jack Charlton took over the managership of the squad in 1986, The Republic of Ireland have grown steadily into an international force to be reckoned with. In 1988 they reached the finals of the European Championships for the first time in their history. And they acquitted themselves with honour, beating England, drawing with the USSR and losing to Holland.

Now, with another touch of irony, the World Cup draw has again lined the Republic alongside England and Holland.

The current squad is comprised of players from the English, Scottish, Spanish and French leagues - but none from the Irish League. This is not unusual, since Ireland has traditionally exported her finest footballing talent across the Irish Sea. Some Irish internationals were not even born in Ireland,

Left: Jack Charlton, the Republic's manager won World Cup honours with England in 1966. Above: Ray Houghton scored against England in their European Championship clash in '88. Can he repeat the feat in Italy 1990?

but represent the country via the parentage ruling. Several don't even speak with an Irish accent! But they are ALL proud to pull on those famous green shirts.

The Republic of Ireland squad for Italia '90 will probably include: *Pat Bonner* (Celtic), *Gerry Peyton* (Bournemouth), *Chris Morris* (Celtic), *Mick McCarthy* (Lyon), *Kevin Moran* (Sporting Gijon), *Steve Staunton, Ray Houghton* (Liverpool), *David O'Leary* (Arsenal), *Paul McGrath* (Aston Villa), *Kevin Sheedy* (Everton), *Ronnie Whelan* (Liverpool), *Andy Townsend* (Norwich), *Frank Stapleton* (Blackburn), *Tony Cascarino* (Millwall), *Tony Galvin* (Swindon), *John Aldridge* (Real Sociedad), *John Byrne* (Le Havre), *Niall Quinn* (Arsenal).

If those lads can take football's most famous trophy back to Dublin, they will rank among the most notable Irish heroes of all time - and Jack Charlton will become King Jack!

John Aldridge will spearhead the Republic's challenge in Italy and all Ireland will hope that he can repeat his club scoring record at international level.

Complete the panel when the actual Rep. of Ireland Squad is announced

1.		13.
2.		14.
3.		15.
4.		16.
5.		17.
6.		18.
7.		19.
8.		20.
9.		21.
10.		22.
11.		23.
12.		24.

1990 marks Romania's fifth World Cup qualification. Their first appearance was at the inaugural tournament way back in 1930 when they were one of only four European nations taking part. They were knocked-out by Uruguay in the opening round.

In Italy in 1934 Romania again went out in the first round, to Czechoslovakia. Cuba were their first round victors in France in 1936. And in 1970 it was a similar story with Romania finishing next to last in their first round group in Mexico.

Since then European soccer has witnessed the rise of the country's two leading clubs, Steaua Bucharest and Dinamo Bucharest. Indeed, Steaua became the first Eastern European club to win the European Cup when they defeated Barcelona (on penalties) in 1986. Later that season they went on to win the European Super Cup with a 1-0 defeat of Cup-Winners Cup holders, Dynamo Kiev.

This success at club level has subsequently given a boost to the national side, with the majority of players in the squad drawn from Steaua and Dinamo.

Romania reached the World Cup Finals by winning a close-run race in the European Qualifying Group One. They pipped Group favourites Denmark by a single point, and decisively settled the campaign in the last game with a 3-1 victory over the Danes.

Now they face an uphill battle in Italy, having been drawn in Group B along with World Champions Argentina, European Championship runners-up USSR and Cameroon, arguably the strongest of the 'minnow' nations.

Nevertheless, look out for veteran goal-getter Rodian Camataru and the gifted attacking midfielder Gheorghe Hagi - if they are on top form then Romanian football could continue its rise in the world game.

Gheorghe Hagi (yellow shirt) Romania's gifted attacking midfielder.

Group B

National Colours: *Yellow shirts, blue shorts, red socks.*

Change Colours: *Blue shirts, yellow shorts, red socks.*

National Stadium: *23rd August Stadium, Bucharest.*

European Qualifying Group One

	P	W	D	L	F	A	Pts
ROMANIA	6	4	1	1	10	5	9
Denmark	6	3	2	1	15	6	8
Greece	6	1	2	3	3	15	4
Bulgaria	6	1	1	4	6	8	3

Romania

Scotland

Group C

National Colours: *Dark blue shirts with white trim, white shorts, red socks.*

Change Colours: *White, yellow and blue hooped shirts, dark blue shorts, white socks with red trim.*

National Stadium: *Hampden Park, Glasgow.*

European Qualifying Group Five

	P	W	D	L	F	A	Pts
Yugoslavia	8	6	2	0	16	6	14
SCOTLAND	8	4	2	2	12	12	10
France	8	3	3	2	10	7	9
Norway	8	2	2	4	10	9	6
Cyprus	8	0	1	7	6	20	1

Opposite page: Mo Johnston scores with a spectacular overhead kick in Scotland's win over Cyprus at Hampden Park during a World Cup qualifying match.
Right: Jim Leighton Scotland's first choice goalkeeper - pointing the way to World Cup success?

Just before half-time in their final World Cup qualifying match against Norway, Ally McCoist put Scotland 1-0 ahead. It was a brilliantly taken goal, an elegant chip over the advancing 'keeper. The scoreline remained the same until the dying seconds of the game when Erland Johnsen unleashed a long range shot at the Scottish goal. The ball struck Jim Leighton awkwardly, he could not control it and it finished up in the net: 1-1. Moments later the Polish referee blew for time and the 64,000 fans packed into Hampden Park breathed a collective sigh of relief. Scotland had got the draw they needed and had made it to Italy.

The matter could have been settled in their favour in either of the previous two qualifying matches. But three agonisingly unfortunate own-goals - two against Yugoslavia, one against France - had helped keep the outcome in the balance. And in keeping with tradition, Scotland had held the fans in suspense right up to the very last minute!

But that's all over now and Scotland have qualified for their fifth World Cup in succession - a record unequalled in the history of the tournament. Yet, on each of the previous four occasions they have never progressed beyond the preliminary round in the finals. Can they do better at Italia '90?

Manager Andy Roxburgh (a former schoolmaster and sometime player with Queen's Park, Falkirk, Partick Thistle and Clydebank) certainly has enough talented players available to him.

His squad, while being without any recognised stars in the mould of a Denis Law, a Billy Bremner, a Graeme

31

Scotland's Paul McStay seen here during his side's 3-1 defeat at the hands of Yugoslavia. He could be a key figure in his country's bid for honours in Italy.

Souness or a Kenny Dalglish, is nevertheless built on solid foundations of hard work and enthusiasm. Perhaps Roxburgh's emphasis on the over-riding importance of teamwork will at last provide the key to success for Scotland.

The squad will probably include: *Jim Leighton* (Man. Utd.), *Andy Goram* (Hibs.), *Maurice Malpas* (Dundee United), *Willie Miller* (Aberdeen), *Alex McLeish* (Aberdeen), *Roy Aitken* (Celtic), *David McPherson* (Hearts), *Steve Nicol* (Liverpool), *Paul McStay* (Celtic), *Jim Bett* (Aberdeen), *Brian McClair* (Man. Utd.), *Murdo Macleod* (Borussia Dortmund), *Stuart McCall* (Everton), *Davie Cooper* (Motherwell), *Pat Nevin* (Everton), *Mo Johnston* (Rangers), *Ally McCoist* (Rangers), *Alan McInally* (Bayern Munich).

The Scots will certainly need strength and skill in every department if they are to overcome strong Group C contenders Sweden and Brazil. Indeed, this will be Scotland's third World Cup Finals encounter with Brazil and they have never beaten them.

But there is a first time for everything!

Complete the panel when the actual Scotland Squad is announced.

1.	13.
2.	14.
3.	15.
4.	16.
5.	17.
6.	18.
7.	19.
8.	20.
9.	21.
10.	22.
11.	23.
12.	24.

South Korea

Group E

National Colours: *All red.*

National Stadium: *Seoul Municipal.*

Final Asian Qualifying Group

	P	W	D	L	F	A	Pts
SOUTH KOREA	5	3	2	0	5	1	8
U.A.E.	5	1	4	0	4	3	6
Qatar	5	1	3	1	4	5	5
China	5	2	0	3	5	6	4
Saudi Arabia	5	1	2	2	4	5	4
North Korea	5	1	1	3	2	4	3

The South Koreans will be making their third trip to a World Cup Finals tournament.

In 1954, in Switzerland, they lost 9-0 to Hungary and 7-0 to Turkey before catching the early flight home.

It was a different story in 1986, in Mexico. This time South Korea managed a draw with Bulgaria and two highly creditable performances against Argentina (lost 2-1) and Italy (lost 3-2), before crashing out of the tournament.

Now, having dominated the Asian qualifying tournament - ahead of the United Arab Emirates (who also qualify for Italy), Quatar, China, Saudia Arabia and North Korea - the South Koreans are back, hoping to improve on past performances.

That will be easier said than done, especially since they've been drawn in the same group as Belgium, Uruguay and Spain. But look out for goal-getters Choi Soon-ho, Hwang Bo-Kwang and Hwang Seon-Hong.

Hwang Bo-Kwang (left) South Korea's talented goal-scorer takes on the Saudi defence during their World Cup qualifying match.

33

Spain boasts one of the finest domestic tournaments in the world with clubs like Real Madrid, Barcelona, Atletico Madrid, Real Sociedad and Athletic Bilbao leading the way. The national side became European Champions in 1964 and were runners-up - to France - in 1984.

And yet, the Spanish have never done particularly well in World Cup competitions. In 1950, when the Championship was decided on a league basis, they reached the final pool but finished fourth with just a single point to show for their efforts. As the host nation in 1982 they got to the second phase but progressed no further. And in 1986 they reached the quarter-finals in Mexico where they were beaten 5-4 after a penalty shoot-out with Belgium.

This time around Spain are determined to do better. They were in fact among the earliest qualifiers, chalking up an impressive 10 points and 14 goals in their first five games in the European Group Six campaign. A further point, earned against Hungary, was enough to make their position virtually unassailable. In their last qualifying game the Spanish really enjoyed themselves with an emphatic 4-0 defeat of Hungary - a result which underlined the Spanish claim to be seeded ahead of England in the finals. However, that situation was resolved in England's favour.

In Italy much will depend on the fitness of superstriker Emilio Butragueno - known affectionately as 'The Vulture' thanks to his habit of swooping in to snap-up the slightest chance. He spent three weeks out of the game with an ankle injury at the beginning of the '89-90 season, but once recovered he was quickly on the scoresheet again for his club Real Madrid.

Spain's star line-up also includes 'keeper Andoni Zubizarreta, of Barcelona, the Real Madrid defenders Manuel Sanchis and Miguel Tendillo and classy right-midfielder Miguel Michel.

It's about time Spain performed well on the World Cup stage. But they are in a tough group and will need to pull out all the stops.

A jubilant Miquel Michel, Spain's classy midfield general, celebrates his goal in his side's 4-0 victory over Malta.

Spain

Group E

National colours: *Red shirts with yellow trim, blue shorts, black socks with yellow trim.*

Change Colours: *Blue shirts, dark blue shorts, black socks*

National Stadia: *Nou Camp, Barcelona and Bernabeu, Madrid*

European Qualifying Group Six

	P	W	D	L	F	A	Pts
SPAIN	8	6	1	1	20	3	13
Rep. of Ireland	8	5	2	1	10	2	12
Hungary	8	2	4	2	8	12	8
N. Ireland	8	2	1	5	6	12	5
Malta	8	0	2	6	3	18	2

Sweden

Group C

National Colours: *Yellow shirts, blue shorts, yellow and blue socks.*

Change Colours: *Blue shirts, white shorts, yellow socks.*

National Stadium: *Fotbollstadion, Solna.*

European Qualifying Group Two

	P	W	D	L	F	A	Pts
SWEDEN	6	4	2	0	9	3	10
England	6	3	3	0	10	0	9
Poland	6	2	1	3	4	8	5
Albania	6	0	0	6	3	15	0

Despite their failure to reach the 1988 European Championships, there has recently been an upsurge of interest in Swedish football.

Indeed, they are currently one of Europe's top teams - with a splendid defence built around the partnership of Glen Hysen and Peter Larsson, and attacking flair in the form of Johnny Ekstrom and Mats Magnusson.

With a splendid 2-0 away victory over Poland they pipped England to first place in the European Group Two qualifying competition. It was a result which caused the World Cup organisers quite a problem as it brought about the seeding controversy between Spain and England.

Although drawn in a tough group - with Brazil and Scotland, the Swedes could prove one of the surprises of the summer.

Don't write them off!

Sweden's stylish defender, Glen Hysen (above), forms a solid defensive partnership with Peter Larsson.

U.A.E.

Group D
National Colours: *All White.*

Final Asian Qualifying Group

	P	W	D	L	F	A	Pts
South Korea	5	3	2	0	5	1	8
U.A.E.	5	1	4	0	4	3	6
Qatar	5	1	3	1	4	5	5
China	5	2	0	3	5	6	4
Saudi Arabia	5	1	2	2	4	5	4
North Korea	5	1	1	3	2	4	3

The United Arab Emirates qualified for Italia '90 by finishing second to South Korea in the 'round robin' tournament which eventually decided the Asian entries. In fact, they were the only country to score against South Korea in the entire qualifying competition.

The squad is managed by ex-Brazilian World Cup ace Mario Zagalo (he was involved in all three of Brazil's Championships, as a player in 1958 and 1962 and as manager in 1970). But even Zagalo would be hard pressed to take the UAE much further and has admitted that their qualifying was little short of a miracle. Realistically they haven't a snowball's chance in the desert, of progressing beyond the first phase!

Abdulla Razaq Ibrahim of the U.A.E. takes on Guo Yijun of China.

"Today you have earned the right to dream." That was the verdict of US coach Bob Gansler after his team had qualified for the 1990 World Cup Finals.

The States' last CONCACAF group qualifying game, against Trinidad and Tobago, was an emotional affair played in searing heat amid a Caribbean carnival atmosphere. 37,000 islanders packed into Trinidad's National Stadium in Port of Spain to will their side to its first World Cup Finals: all they needed was a draw. But it wasn't to be - Paul Caligiuri's 31st minute goal for the Americans saw to that. And so the USA claimed the 24th spot at Italia '90.

In terms of prestige and credibility this was considered a vital qualification since the States will host the World Cup Finals in 1994. That honour had been bestowed by FIFA in recognition of the US's proven expertise at organising and marketing other big sporting events, rather than their prowess on the football pitch.

Soccer has so far failed to make much impact on the US sporting scene. The North American Soccer League was a short-lived enterprise which could not compete with the American obsession for baseball and the gridiron game. But with 1994 only four years away, you can be sure that a new league will rise in America.

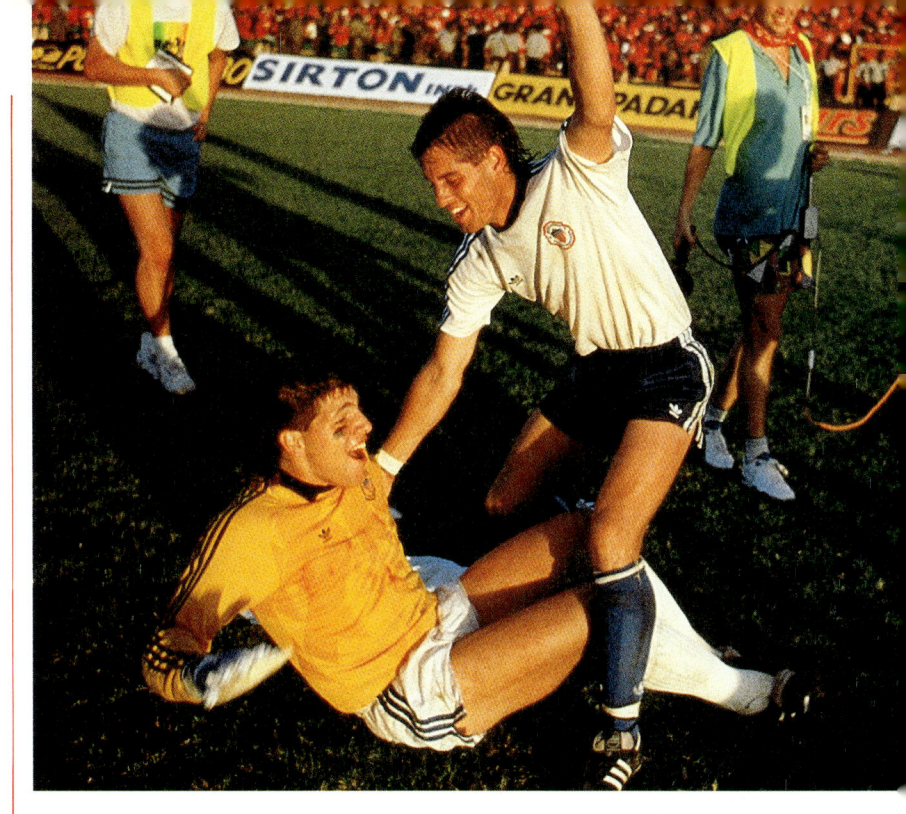

Meanwhile, coach Gansler has his work cut out in preparing his rather ordinary squad to meet the elite of world football. One solution he is currently considering involves inviting certain 'stateless' players to join the team. Queen's Park Rangers striker Roy Wegerle - born in South Africa, married to an American and apparently keen to become an American citizen - is reportedly top of Gansler's list. Wegerle, and players like him, would be a valuable asset to American ambitions. The USA will certainly need all the help it can get in facing up to the might of Italy, Austria and Czechoslovakia.

Whatever happens in 1990, the USA will undoubtedly use the experience as a springboard to 1994. After all, they have already qualified for that tournament.

John Harkes and Tony Meola of the USA celebrate their history making victory over Trinidad and Tobago.

Group A

National Colours: *White shirts, blue shorts, red socks.*

CONCACAF Qualifying Group

	P	W	D	L	F	A	Pts
Costa Rica	8	5	1	2	10	8	11
U.S.A.	8	4	3	1	6	3	11
Trinidad & Tobago	8	3	3	2	7	5	9
Guatemala	6	1	1	4	4	7	3*
El Salvador	6	0	2	4	2	8	2*

* Guatemala and El Salvador did not complete their programme of matches

Of all the twenty-four nations competing in Italia '90, Uruguay must be wishing more than most for a return to past glories. For they were the winners of the first World Cup way back in 1930, when they beat Argentina 4-2 in the final.

Twenty-years later Uruguay lifted the trophy for the second time, by topping the final 'pool' ahead of Brazil, Sweden and Spain. In 1954, in Switzerland, they reached the semi-final where they lost 4-2 to Hungary in what is still regarded as one of the finest football matches of all time.

Since those glory days Uruguay have languished in the shadow of South American neighbours Brazil and Argentina. And along the way they have also gained something of a reputation for rough, tough, uncompromising play.

It is this image that manager Washington Tabarez would now like to see banished forever. He wants the modern Uruguay to be remembered for the fine football of which he knows they are more than capable.

Superstars Enzo Francescoli and Ruben Sosa will be among the players attempting to restore Uruguay's footballing pride.

South American superstar, Ruben Sosa, will be attempting to restore Uruguay's pride and reputation in Italy 1990.

Group E

National Colours: *Sky blue shirts, black shorts, black socks with sky blue trim*

National Stadium: *Centenary, Montevideo.*

South American Qualifying Group One

	P	W	D	L	F	A	Pts
URUGUAY	4	3	0	1	7	2	6
Bolivia	4	3	0	1	6	5	6
Peru	4	0	0	4	2	8	0

Uruguay

Group C

National Colours: *Red shirts, white shorts, red socks.*

Change Colours: *All white.*

National Stadia: *Dynamo Stadium, Moscow and Kirov Stadium, Leningrad.*

European Qualifying Group Three

	P	W	D	L	F	A	Pts
USSR	8	4	3	1	11	4	11
Austria	8	3	3	2	9	9	9
Turkey	8	3	1	4	12	10	7
E. Germany	8	3	1	4	9	13	7
Iceland	8	1	4	3	6	11	6

USSR

In the summer of 1988 the USSR finished as runners-up to Holland in the European Championships, thereby confounding the critics who had previously written them off as a team of also-rans. In the semi-final they beat Italy 2-0 with a superb all-round team performance that was admired throughout the world of football.

Now, despite a faltering start with a 1-1 draw against Iceland in Reykjavic, the Russians have won through to the World Cup Finals by topping the European Qualifying Group Three table. And in Italy this summer they will quietly assert themselves as one of the strongest contenders in the competition.

They certainly have the talent to do well against the world's finest. It begins right at the back with Rinat Dasayev, arguably the world's No.1 'keeper, and extends through the defence with players like Oleg Kuznetsov and Vladimir Bessonov. The midfield is motivated by Alexander Zavarov, Gennadi Litovchenko and Alexi Mikhailichenko while the forward department contains the explosive talents of Oleg Protasov and Igor Belanov.

The Russians are coming - and the rest of the world must take note.

The explosive talent of Oleg Protasov is just one of the key factors that could make the USSR a team to watch this summer.

West Germany

Group D

National Colours: *White shirts with black, orange and yellow trim, black shorts, white socks.*

Change Colours: *Green shirts, white shorts, white socks.*

National Stadia: *Olympic Stadium, Berlin; Olympic Stadium, Munich.*

European Qualifying Group Four

	P	W	D	L	F	A	Pts
Holland	6	4	2	0	8	2	10
WEST GERMANY	6	3	3	0	13	3	9
Finland	6	1	1	4	4	16	3
Wales	6	0	2	4	4	8	2

West Germany have been a major presence in the World Cup since 1954 when against all expectations they won the trophy by beating favourites Hungary in the final. In 1958 they finished in fourth place behind Brazil, Sweden and France. They were quarter-finalists in 1962, runners-up in '66 and took third place in 1970. In 1974, as host nation, they won the trophy for the second time in their history, beating Holland 2-1 in a memorable final. 1982 and 1986 saw them as runners-up to Italy and Argentina.

For a nation with such a fine World Cup pedigree, West Germany made surprisingly heavy going of their qualifying campaign for Italia '90. They eventually arrived via the same route as England - as one of the two 'second best' teams in the smaller European qualifying groups.

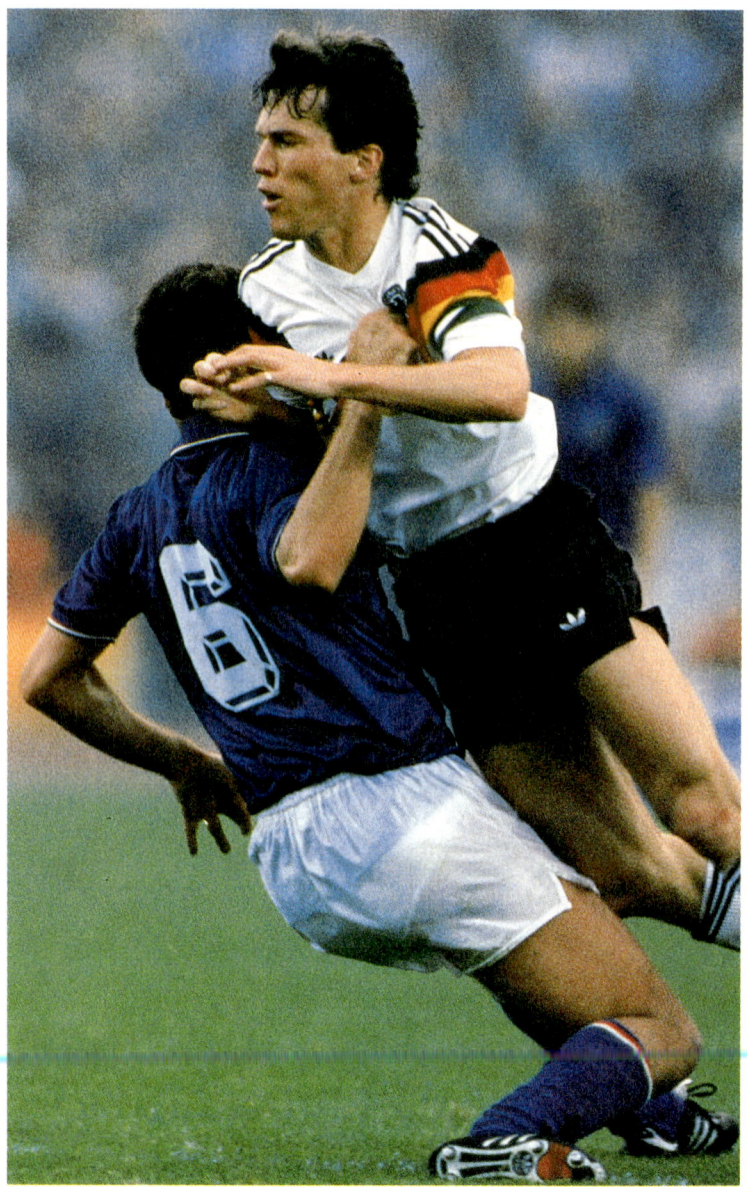

By October 1989 it seemed probable that the West Germans would finish as runners-up to Holland in the European Group Four campaign. But that position wouldn't necessarily be enough to see them through. Their problem was lack of goals. A high goals tally could prove the vital ingredient in the 'second place' qualifying stakes. And until that time they had scored just five times in four games. It was then that Franz Beckenbauer's boys took on Finland, in Dortmund.

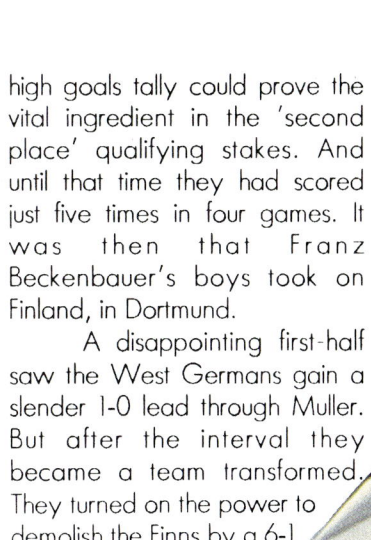

A disappointing first-half saw the West Germans gain a slender 1-0 lead through Muller. But after the interval they became a team transformed. They turned on the power to demolish the Finns by a 6-1 margin, with goals from Littbarski, Klinsmann, Vtller, Matthaus (a penalty) and another from Muller.

"I knew the goals would come," said a relieved, yet proud Beckenbauer after the game. It was a result he badly needed. It certainly did the West German goal-difference figures a power of good, and also served as a timely reminder that West Germany are still a major force in world soccer. In November a 2-1 victory over Wales was enough to secure their place in the finals.

Now West Germany, seeded in Italy on previous World Cup form, should progress well beyond the opening phase.

Opposite page: West Germany's Lothar Matthaus tangles with Italy's Ferri during the Euopean Championships in 1988. Left: Jurgan Klinsmann, his goal-scoring exploits have made him a European Footballer Of The Year.

So far Yugoslavia remain unbeaten in their 1990 World Cup campaign, having won 6 games and drawn 2 to dominate their qualifying group, ahead of Scotland, France, Norway and Cyprus.

In theory this makes them one of the strongest of the European challengers. However, history shows that Yugoslavia has an unfortunate habit of finishing second best when it comes to the big tournaments.

They have twice been runners-up in the European Championship - to Russia in 1960 and to Italy in 1968. Their best effort to date in the World Cup is fourth place (twice) in 1930 and 1962.

In 1987 Yugoslavia won the World Youth Cup in Chile, a feat which augers well for the future. Perhaps 1990 will prove a turning point for the senior squad. They certainly have the potential to qualify from Group D, along with West Germany.

Star-turns to watch out for are midfield aces Safet Sucic and Dragan Stojkovic.

Dragan Stojkovac, Yugoslavia's danger man and one of the most talented players in Europe.

Group D

National colours: *Blue shirts, white shorts, red socks.*

Change Colours: *All white.*

National Stadia: *Red Star, Belgrade* and *Kosevo, Sarajevo*

European Qualifying Group Five

	P	W	D	L	F	A	Pts
YUGOSLAVIA	8	6	2	0	16	6	14
Scotland	8	4	2	2	12	12	10
France	8	3	3	2	10	7	9
Norway	8	2	2	4	10	9	6
Cyprus	8	0	1	7	6	20	1

Yugoslavia

1966 AND ALL THAT

- A World Cup History

Way back in May 1904, four Frenchmen called a meeting in Paris to discuss their proposal for a World Championship of soccer. Also present were representatives from Belgium, Denmark, Holland, Spain and Switzerland. By the end of the proceedings the Federation Internationale de Football Association (FIFA) had been formed - and written into the association's constitution was a clause stating that FIFA held the exclusive right to organise and administer a world tournament. However, a further twenty-six years were to pass before the first World Cup Finals were held.

In the intervening period Jules Rimet and Henri Delaunay - two of FIFA's founding fathers - worked tirelessly to achieve their dream. Their efforts were of course thwarted by the Great War of 1914-18 and it wasn't until the late 1920's that the dream began to look anything like a reality. The case for a professional

A dream come true. The Argentinean goalkeeper, Nery Pumpido, proudly holds aloft the World Cup after his side's 3-2 victory over West Germany in Mexico 1986.

Above: *World Cup Final 1958; Sweden v Brazil. This was the final when a true footballing superstar was born. Pele (dark shirt) scored two memorable goals in his side's 5-2 win over host nation, Sweden.* Below: *Probably the most controversial incident ever in a World Cup Final happened in the 1966 final between England and West Germany at Wembley. The score was 2-2 and the match was into extra-time. Geoff Hurst hammered a shot against the German crossbar. The ball bounced downwards but did it cross the line? The referee consulted his linesman and a goal was given.*

championship was greatly strengthened when football proved to be one of the most popular events in the 1924 and 1928 Olympic Games - with Uruguay winning gold medals on both occasions. And when Rimet suggested to the Uruguayan President that his country should host the first World Cup, the idea was greeted with enthusiasm.

Consequently the first World Cup Finals were held in Montevideo in July 1930. Thirteen nations took part - just four of them from Europe. The early stage of the tournament was played on a league basis with the winners of four groups going through to the semi-finals.

Favourites Uruguay won through to the final, against their traditional rivals Argentina. The match, played at Montevideo's brand new Centenary Stadium in front of a restricted crowd of 90,000, was a truly exciting affair with Uruguay winning 4-2 to become soccer's first World Champions. After the match they were presented with the magnificent gold trophy that was to become the most sought after prize in world soccer.

In 1934 reigning World Champions Uruguay, somewhat aggrieved by the poor turn-out of European competitors at the 1930 event, and affected by a players' strike, did not travel to Italy for the second World Cup Finals.

This time 32 nations took part in a qualifying tournament, sixteen of them eventually making the journey to Italy in May and June 1934. Italy and Czechoslovakia reached the final, played in Rome on June 10. The Czechs took the lead in the 70th minute through left-winger Puc. Twelve minutes later Orsi equalised

44

for Italy with a magnificent curling shot. The game went into extra-time and Schiavo snatched the winner for Italy in the 97th minute.

France were the hosts for the 1938 tournament, played amidst an atmosphere of political uncertainty. Several nations - including Austria, Japan, Bolivia and Mexico - withdrew from the competition while Uruguay and Argentina refused to take part at all.

Despite these setbacks the French staged a splendid World Cup. Italy once again emerged as Champions, beating Hungary 4-2 in the final on June 19.

The outbreak of the Second World War in 1939 put paid to the 1942 Finals which were to have been staged in either Argentina or Brazil.

After the war the FIFA congress sat in 1946 and agreed that the next World Cup would be held in Brazil in 1950 and that its outcome would be decided entirely on a league basis with the winners of four groups playing for points in the final pool. They also decided to officially name the cup 'The Jules Rimet Trophy' in honour of FIFA's President.

England competed in the World Cup for the first time in 1950 and were widely tipped to be up there among the final four. But defeats by Spain and the relatively inexperienced USA meant that the English squad caught the early flight home.

The final pool was contested between Brazil, Spain, Sweden and Uruguay and it all boiled down to the last match of the tournament between Brazil and Uruguay, with Brazil needing no more than a draw to take the trophy.

A record 199,854 fans turned out to see the match in the newly-built Maracana Stadium on July 16. Shortly after half-time Friaca scored to put Brazil in the lead. Schiaffino equalised for Uruguay in the 65th minute and 14 minutes later Ghiggia scored the winner to give Uruguay her second World Cup in just two attempts.

Switzerland hosted the 1954 Finals.

Hungary, the 'Magical Magyars', had recently emerged as a fabulous footballing nation and were firm favourites to win the trophy. And so it was no surprise when they reached the Final in Berne, against West Germany.

However, despite scoring twice in the first ten minutes, through Puskas and Czibor, the Hungarians could not counter the dogged persistence that was (and still is) a feature of their opponents' game. Slowly but surely the Germans got back into the game and drew level with goals by Morlock and Rahn. Then, twelve minutes from time, Rahn scored again to put Germany into the lead. Puskas scored again for Hungary, but the goal was disallowed - and West Germany took the trophy.

The host nation Sweden reached the 1958 final in Stockholm on June 29 - but there they met the formidable Brazilians and a fabulous 18 year-old superstar named Pele. Sweden went ahead in the fourth minute with a low drive from Liedholm. Then Vava scored twice for Brazil.

In the second half the young Pele really made his name when he scored a magnificent goal, first controlling the ball on his thigh, then flicking it over his head before turning to volley past Svensson in the Swedish goal. Zagalo hit Brazil's fourth. Then Sweden pulled one back through Simonsson. But it was Pele who rounded things off by heading Brazil's fifth. Brazil had won the Jules Rimet Trophy for the first time.

The 1962 tournament was staged in Chile and once again Brazil reached the final. This time their opponents were Czechoslovakia, making their second attempt to win the World Cup. The match was played in Santiago on June 17.

Masopust opened the scoring for Czechoslovakia in the 15th minute. Three minutes later Amarildo - standing in for the injured Pele - scored a fabulous equaliser with a curling shot from a seemingly impossible angle. Late second half goals by Zito and Vava ensured that the trophy stayed with Brazil.

Before 1966 England had never done particularly well in the World Cup - their best attempts had taken them only as far as the quarter-finals in 1954 and 1962. Indeed, the English squad had not been a major force in the world game since the famous 6-3 defeat by the Hungarian maestros in 1953.

All that was about to change.

The '66 finals were staged in England - but amazingly they almost began without the prized Jules Rimet Trophy! The trophy was stolen from Westminster's Central Hall where it had been on display. The police and the Football Association were baffled, it looked as if the most famous statuette in world football had vanished off the face of the earth. But, one week after the theft, a small black-and-white dog named Pickles was taking his master for a walk in Norwood, South-London, when he began digging in the undergrowth and came up with some buried treasure - the World Cup, wrapped up in brown paper! Pickles' owner collected a £6,000 reward, the dog became a canine celebrity and the tournament went ahead as planned.

Pressing the home advantage Alf Ramsey's England forced their way into the final. En route they topped their group ahead of Uruguay and then went on to dispose of Argentina in the quarter-finals and Portugal in the semis.

And so 100,000 spectators at Wembley Stadium and millions of TV viewers around the world witnessed England's finest footballing hour on July 30. Opponents West Germany opened the scoring in the 13th minute with a goal by Haller who pounced on a mistake by full-back Ray Wilson. Six minutes later Geoff Hurst headed in England's equaliser.

It looked as though England had wrapped things up in the 78th minute when Martin Peters' shot beat Tilkowski in the German goal. But there was more drama to come when,

Above: Gerb Muller, scorer of West Germany's winning goal in the 1974 final against Holland, shows off the trophy. Below: An inspired Brazil, with Pele in brilliant form, captured the World Cup for a record third time when they beat Italy 4-1 in Mexico 1970.

in the last minute of normal time, Weber equalised for West Germany.

The thirty minutes of extra-time that followed must rank among the most exciting and the most controversial in the history of football.

Inspired by Alf Ramsey's pep talk England fought like lions to regain the lead. It came in the 100th minute: Geoff Hurst met an Alan Ball cross, then he turned and hammered the ball goalwards. It struck the underside of the bar and rebounded downwards. The Swiss referee consulted the Russian linesman and he raised his flag to signify that it was a goal.

There was even more excitement to come. In the last minute a Bobby Moore clearance out of defence found Geoff Hurst who unleashed a 20 yard shot which secured his hat-trick and sealed the victory for England.

Brazil came back with a bang in the 1970 competition, staged in Mexico. With the great Pele as their inspiration the Brazilians produced magnificent, fluent football that was a joy to watch. Brushing aside Czechoslovakia, England, Romania, Peru and Uruguay they reached the final - played at the Aztec Stadium in Mexico City on June 21. Their opponents were Italy, a team whose success had been built on the solid foundations of a firm defence. A fascinating battle was in prospect.

In the event the silky skills of the Brazilians proved too much for the iron will of Italy. It was a dazzling display which fully justified the 4-1 scoreline. Brazil's goals came from Pele, Gerson, Jairzinho and Carlos Alberto. Boninsenga replied for Italy. In honour of Brazil's third World Cup Final win, the Jules Rimet Trophy became their permanent property.

A new trophy - the FIFA World Cup - was the prize in the 1974 tournament, staged in West Germany. This time the host nation reached the final, against neighbouring Holland. The match was played in Munich on July 7.

In the opening minute, and without a German player having touched the ball, Neeskens converted a penalty for Holland. But West Germany soon got into their stride and when they were awarded a penalty, Breitner levelled the score. The game was all wrapped up in the 43rd minute when Muller scored West Germany's second.

Holland reached their second consecutive World Cup Final in 1978. Again their opponents were the host nation, this time Argentina. The match, played in Buenos Aires on June 25, was a patchy affair, characterised by a string of cynical fouls. Kempes scored first for Argentina in the 38th minute. Substitute Nanninga equalised for Holland with just seven minutes to go. This took the game into extra-time during which further goals from Kempes and Bertoni made Argentina World Champions for the first time.

Sunny Spain hosted the 1982 competition. The final was played in Madrid on July 11. Italy became only the second nation to win the World Cup three times with a convincing 3-1 victory over West Germany. Rossi, Tardelli and Altobelli scored for Italy; Breitner for West Germany.

In 1986 Mexico became the first nation to twice host the World Cup. Argentina, inspired by the magical Maradona, won through to the final against West Germany. The game, played in Mexico City on June 29, was an exciting one with the Germans fighting back to equalise after being 0-2 down. Brown and Valdano had scored for Argentina; Rummenigge and Voller for West Germany. Then, with six minutes of the match remaining Maradona split the German defence with a stunning pass to Burruchaga who blasted in the winner.

Which nation will write the next chapter in the history of the World Cup?

WORLD CUP FINALS

URUGUAY 1930
Uruguay 4, Argentina 2
ITALY 1934
Italy 2, Czechoslovakia 1 (aet)
FRANCE 1938
Italy 4, Hungary 2
BRAZIL 1950
Uruguay 2, Brazil 1
SWITZERLAND 1954
West Germany 3, Hungary 2
SWEDEN 1958
Brazil 5, Sweden 2
CHILE 1962
Brazil 3, Czechoslovakia 1
ENGLAND 1966
England 4, West Germany 2 (aet)
MEXICO 1970
Brazil 4, Italy 1
WEST GERMANY 1974
West Germany 2, Holland 1
ARGENTINA 1978
Argentina 3, Holland 1 (aet)
SPAIN 1982
Italy 3, West Germany 1
MEXICO 1986
Argentina 3, West Germany 2

GREAT WORLD CUP COMPETITION

3 PORTABLE COLOUR TVs TO BE WON!

Yes, *YOU* could see all the excitement and drama of the World Cup unfold on your very own super 14 inch colour television!

All you have to do is answer our six World Cup questions, write the answers in the correct order on a postcard or sealed envelope along with your name, address and age. Then send your entry to:

*Grandreams/World Cup Competition
Jadwin House,
205-211 Kentish Town Road,
London, NW5 2JU*

1
Who was the leading goalscorer in the 1986 World Cup Finals?
2
For how many successive World Cup finals have Scotland qualified?
3
In which year did Jack Charlton win a World Cup winners' medal?
4
Where will the 1990 World Cup Final be played?
5
Name the dog who found the missing World Cup in 1966?
6
Where will the 1994 World Cup Finals be staged?

Entries must be received no later than April 30, 1990.

The senders of the first 3 correct entries drawn from all those received will each win a fabulous 14 inch colour tv. The editor's decision is final. No correspondence will be entered into.